WALKING

THE_ EARTH

Donated in Memory

of our son

Timothy Ahearn

WALKING THE_ EARTH

The History of Human Migration

Tricia Andryszewski

TF
CB
Twenty-First Century Books • **Minneapolis**

For Bridget and Matthew

Twenty-First Century Books
A division of Lerner Publishing Group
241 First Avenue North
Minneapolis, Minnesota 55401 U.S.A.

Website address: www.lernerbooks.com

Library of Congress Cataloging-in-Publication Data

Andryszewski, Tricia, 1956–
    Walking the earth : the history of human migration / by Tricia Andryszewski.
        p.   cm.
    Includes bibliographical references and index.
    ISBN-13: 978–0–7613–3458–3 (lib. bdg. : alk. paper)
    ISBN-10: 0–7613–3458–0 (lib. bdg. : alk. paper)
    1. Human beings–Migrations. 2. Agriculture, Prehistoric. 3. Population. I. Title.
GN370.A53 2007
304.8–dc22   2005033430

Manufactured in the United States of America
1 2 3 4 5 6 – DP – 12 11 10 09 08 07

CONTENTS

Once early humans developed the ability to make primitive tools and use fire, it became easier for them to hunt and prepare food.

chapter one

PREHISTORY

The very first modern humans, *Homo sapiens,* people pretty much like us, lived about 150,000 years ago. Compared to other animals, they (and we) were and are very unusual in several ways. Each of these differences is a key to how humans spread out and grew in number to cover and dominate the entire planet.

The first modern humans inherited from their even more ancient, not-quite-fully-human ancestors a wealth of features that enabled them both to travel far and to adapt to living in strange places. The most important feature is that their brains (like ours) were huge compared to the size of their bodies. They also inherited the ability to eat many different kinds of foods—very important for surviving in places as different as, say, African grassland and Arctic tundra. They inherited the ability to stand and walk on two feet, legs suited for long-distance running and walking, hands free for making and using tools, and brains clever enough to create tools and solve problems. Perhaps equally important, they, like their ancestors, were social animals, so their inheritance include not

WORLD POPULATION

PREHISTORY 10,000 BCE
about 5 million

Two to three million years ago, the earliest humanlike beings, known as *Homo habilis*, evolved to two-legged locomotion while living in the vast African grasslands called savannas.

The brain represents approximately 2 percent of the total body weight of an adult human, making the human brain larger and heavier in comparison to body weight than that of any other animal.

just their physical bodies but also the beginnings of human culture–knowledge about how to use and make a few primitive cutting and spearing and digging tools and (very important) how to use fire. Mastery of fire greatly improved their ability to survive. They used it for warmth and cooking, for driving game animals toward waiting hunters, and to remodel the land around them to better meet their needs.

The land around these first humans was African savanna, grassland with scattered clumps of trees–the ultimate ancestral homeland of us all. It's true that primitive hominids, distant relatives who branched off the human family tree millions of years before *Homo sapiens* existed, migrated out of Africa into Europe and Asia long, long ago, but these are not our ancestors. Every human being alive today, everywhere on Earth, is the great-great-(add about two thousand more greats)-grandchild of someone who lived on African savanna 60,000 years ago.

Are We at All Neanderthal?

Neanderthals (*Homo neanderthalensis*), *right,* were primitive humans who branched off the proto-human family tree long before *Homo sapiens* did and migrated out of Africa long before the great migration of *Homo sapiens* out of Africa began. Neanderthals and their distant *Homo sapiens* cousins both lived in Europe for a time, about 35,000 years ago. Could they have met? Yes. Did they mingle and make families together? Perhaps. Are modern Europeans partly descended from Neanderthals? Nobody knows—but if so, scientists agree, the Neanderthal contribution to the genes of modern humans is invisibly small. What we do know is that as *Homo sapiens* established themselves throughout Europe, the number of Neanderthals dwindled, most likely because *Homo sapiens* were gobbling up most of the Neanderthals' food supply.

Between 150,000 years ago and about 100,000 years ago, *Homo sapiens*, each and 11
every one, lived in Africa. There we prospered and grew enough to manage the single
most important cultural development in human history: language.

Many different kinds of animals, from chipmunks to eagles, make noises that
have meaning–alarm calls, songs to attract mates, sounds that say, "Where's my
mom?" What makes human language different is that we use combinations of sounds
as symbols, and their meaning depends on their
order: "man bites dog" has a different meaning than
"dog bites man." With every language, all over the
world, human children learn this when they're two
years old. Scientists believe that the very first humans
to learn this did so sometime before about 60,000
years ago, in Africa.

It's often said that language is what makes
humans human, different from animals. But language is
just one of a cluster of uniquely human phenomena that
probably began together, intermingled and
interdependent. Song and dance have been found in
every human community everywhere on Earth, and it
makes sense that the first people to speak also sang and
danced. Song and dance are powerful aids in
remembering stories, in rehearsing and teaching
cooperative behavior, and in encouraging emotional
bonds. Certainly, humans became artists around the time
they adopted language–bits of artwork that old have
been found by archaeologists. It also makes sense that

This is a model of a
Homo sapiens man.
Modern humans are
characterized by the
lighter build of their
skeletons compared to
earlier humans. Modern
humans also have a very
large brain in a high,
vaulted cranium with a
flat, almost vertical
forehead.

12 humans have been religious for just as long: In every human community, we find belief in a spirit world, invisible but real in its effects on the physical world and open to interaction with humans.

The impact of language was huge, for language made it possible for humans to share information with each other in ways far beyond what animals can manage. It made it possible for humans to know about and benefit from experiences they'd never had themselves. It became possible, for example, to learn that a particular plant was poisonous just by talking with someone who ate it, rather than by finding out the hard way by eating it yourself. Language enabled better food gathering, as people could now share their knowledge about which parts of what plants were edible, where and when foods grew and became ripe for eating, and how to cook or otherwise prepare them to make them edible and nourishing. Language enabled better cooperation, so that groups of people could together do a better job than loners could do in gathering food, in hunting, and in surviving everything from bad weather to attacks by wild animals.

Language also enabled better tool making, as people shared detailed and specific information about, say, how exactly to make the best digging stick for getting at a certain kind of root, or how to make a more forceful spear. The development of better hunting tools was especially important, for such tools made high-protein, nourishing meat more available to humans. Better weaponry like the bow and arrow better enabled humans to kill prey at a distance, which both expanded a hunter's

Family Tree In April 2005, the National Geographic Society began a five-year project aimed at sorting out the world's largest family tree, or genealogy. Blood samples were to be collected from 100,000 indigenous (native) peoples around the world. Scientists plan to analyze the samples' genetic material. They hope to learn from it more about when and where peoples from around the world shared common ancestors. They also expect to learn more about the sequence of migratory routes followed out of Africa and around the world thousands of years ago.

reach and made it much less likely that hunters would be injured fighting a wild animal. Avoiding injury was very, very important in ancient times. Before the invention of antibiotics and other modern medicine, infection from minor injuries was often fatal.

Altogether, this language-enabled explosion of human development vastly improved humans' chances of survival. *Homo sapiens* not only survived, they thrived. More and more survived to adulthood and successfully raised children—and more and more of their children survived, too. When the number of humans living in a particular place grew large enough that the local supply of food couldn't feed them all, they spread out into new places. Not every band of early humans who moved beyond familiar territory survived. But enough did that, bit by bit, the best hunting and foraging locations in and near African savannas became filled with thousands of people. And we didn't stop there.

Over the next 50,000 years, humans on the move from our original African homeland peopled every corner of Earth short of Antarctica. How do we know this? Ancient people tens of thousands of years ago didn't leave behind any written record of their travels—and certainly no photographs or computer files. Researchers use several different kinds of tools that help them make guesses about ancient human history. When different kinds of tools point to the same guess, it's a good bet that guess is correct.

The most basic set of these tools is archaeological. We dig up the spearheads and firepits and trash at sites where humans lived long ago, compare them with what we find at other sites, and try to figure out when the sites were occupied. We can guess pretty well about this because all living beings leave certain traces in the atoms of their physical remains that change at a steady rate long after the plant or animal dies. Scientists can tell the age of a bit of ancient plant or animal matter from its state of change.

14   Another set of tools for dating human migration looks at language. The pattern of which languages are related to which other languages, and how closely, gives us a pretty good sense of where the people who first spoke these languages migrated in ancient times.

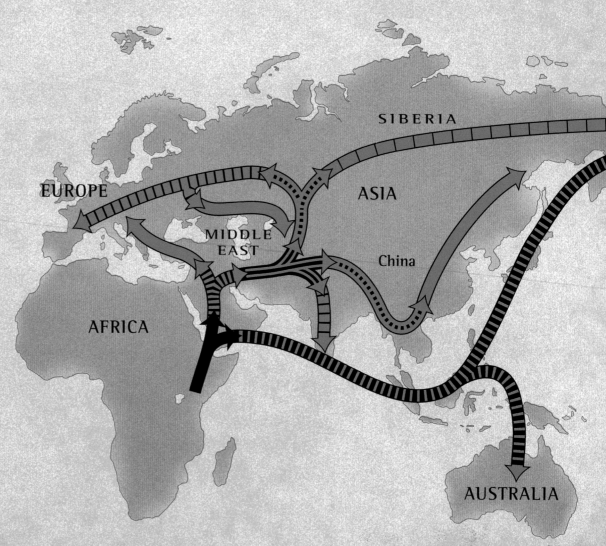

Source: Spencer Wells, *The Journey of Man: A Genetic Odyssey* (Princeton, NJ: Princeton University Press, 2002), 182–183.

Most recently, since the 1980s, scientists have traced and dated ancient
migration patterns with a new set of tools using modern human DNA, the genetic code
we inherit from our parents. Each of us has a unique set of genes, a combination of
those of our parents, written in a chemical called DNA (deoxyribonucleic acid). In

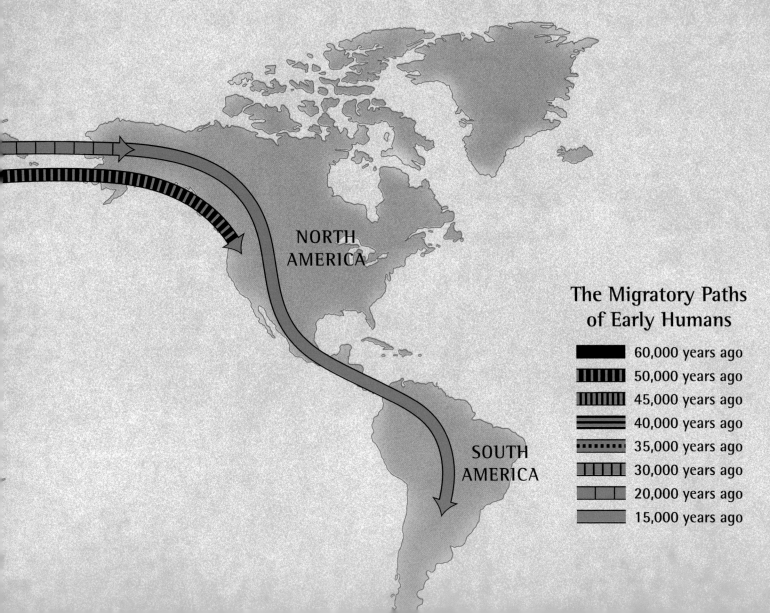

NORTH
AMERICA

SOUTH
AMERICA

The Migratory Paths of Early Humans

▬▬▬	60,000 years ago
▐▐▐▐	50,000 years ago
▐▐▐▐	45,000 years ago
▬▬▬	40,000 years ago
▪▪▪▪▪	35,000 years ago
▐▐▐▐	30,000 years ago
▐ ▐ ▐	20,000 years ago
▬▬▬	15,000 years ago

16   passing genes from generation to generation, sometimes our bodies make errors in copying, called mutations. Some mutations are so bad that the person who has them doesn't survive to have children and pass those genes on to future generations. A very few mutations are so good, giving such an advantage to those who have them, that they spread rapidly through the human family and increase greatly in future generations. Most mutations make no practical difference at all, but are nonetheless passed on. By looking for copies of these make-no-difference mutations in modern DNA (especially the DNA of the Y chromosome and the mitochondria, which mutate at a steady, clocklike rate and avoid the reshuffling that other genes undergo in sexual reproduction), we can see which modern people share ancient ancestors. As researchers have found and compared dozens of these mutations in people all over the world—and compared that evidence with the archaeological and language evidence—a pattern of who moved where and when has emerged.

> **Some mutations are so bad that the person who has them doesn't survive to have children and pass those genes on to future generations.**

The patterns of mutation in modern human DNA, confirmed by the other evidence, clearly point back to common ancestors for all of us in Africa. These patterns also tell us about migration. Most aboriginal Australians, for example, share a particular mutation that is also common among coastal south Asians—but very rare anyplace else in the world, including Africa. This suggests that the ancestors of aboriginal Australians (1) left Africa, for they share the basic African genes we all do, (2) followed a coastal route out of Africa toward Asia, (3) unknowingly created and spread among themselves a mutation that would become their genetic signature, and (4) then carried that mutation with them along the south Asian coast and into Australia.

The routes these early migrants took, to Australia and elsewhere around the world, were arranged by landscape and climate features. The first people to see the Himalaya Mountains, for example, didn't go up over their harsh, frozen peaks but instead migrated through the lowlands around them, where food opportunities and weather were better. Over the tens of thousands of years of this first great migration from Africa to the rest of the world, climate conditions changed in some of the places where humans lived. Some African grassland slowly became desert, for example, ultimately forcing the people who lived there to move on. And at a critical moment during the most recent ice age, dry land emerged between the lands we now call Siberia and Alaska, making overland human migration to the Americas possible. (What we call the Ice Age was really only the most recent of many ice ages, as Earth's climate has naturally alternated between thousands of years of cold weather and thousands of years of the kind of warmer weather we've had in recent times.)

The greatest advantage, though, was that cold places have more large animals, since big body size helps an animal get through cold winters.

The early migrants lacked maps showing them what lay beyond where they could see or had previously lived. Only bands of people lucky enough to move to places that favored their needs managed to survive. Surprisingly, successful migration routes often led from warm, tropical Africa to much colder parts of the world. Cold places presented obvious challenges, met more or less well by human ingenuity, such as keeping warm with fire or animal pelts. But cold places also presented advantages. For example, many of the infectious disease germs and parasites that had co-evolved with humans in tropical Africa couldn't survive much cold.

The greatest advantage, though, was that cold places have more large animals, since big body size helps an animal get through cold winters. Bigger game animals were

Mastodon remains have been associated with fires, leading to the assumption that early humans hunted and ate the large animals.

a big help to early humans, who depended on hunting for much or most of their food. As humans migrated to new, colder places, they encountered large animals–megafauna–that had never before seen humans and didn't know to be afraid of them: Why would an enormous mastodon that's never seen a spear be afraid of such small and apparently weak creatures as humans? When mastodons ignored human newcomers, humans killed the unwary beasts and feasted.

From Australia to the Americas, dozens of species of megafauna died out and became extinct not long after the first humans arrived among them. Did early human hunters kill them off? It's hard to tell. During the tens of thousands of years when humans were first spreading out around the planet, Earth's climate went through changes that probably also contributed to the extinction of large animals. Large animals need a lot of food, and climate change can make food supplies unreliable.

The megafauna extinction is just part of a much bigger story. All over the world, from the first humans in Africa to all of us today, people have adapted themselves to live in whatever environment they find themselves in. We've also changed our environments, for example, by burning brush to improve hunting and by killing off game. As we've changed our environments, we've further adapted our ways of living to cope with the changes. This sometimes dangerous dance of nature and culture continues to this day.

People have adapted themselves to live in whatever environment they find themselves in.

We can best see how this worked during the great migration out of Africa by looking at specific people in a specific place. Consider, for example, the Clovis people. (Their name comes from the town of Clovis, New Mexico, near where archaeologists first dug up some of the distinctive stone spearheads made only by them.) Beginning about 13,200 years ago and continuing for only about three hundred years, the Clovis people left spearheads scattered over much of what is now the United States and Mexico. By the end of that time, megafauna that had lived in America during the Ice Age—mastodons, woolly mammoths, giant bears and bison and cats—were extinct, having failed to survive the double whammy of warmer weather and human hunting.

So what did the Clovis people do? The few hundred or few thousand of their ancestors who had crossed over into America from Siberia had eaten well enough from the

The Clovis people, a group of Paleo-Indians, were among the first human inhabitants of the Americas. Paleo-Indians are ancestors of all the indigenous cultures of North and South America. A hallmark of the Clovis culture is their distinctively shaped, fluted rock spear point.

megafauna they hunted to quickly increase in population enough to spread out across America. When the megafauna were gone, the people who had hunted them had to change the way they lived to adapt to that change in their environment. How they changed varied depending on where they lived. Successful survival strategies in what is now New Mexico, for example, had to be different from what worked, say, on the Pacific Coast.

In New Mexico, the rapid population growth of the megafauna hunting era stopped, and the number of people living there remained about the same for thousands of years. Probably no more than two thousand to six thousand people lived in all of New Mexico between 12,000 and 7,000 years ago. They still hunted, but the game was smaller and wilier and supported fewer people than the megafauna had. Then, about 7,000 years ago, the climate shifted further, becoming even warmer and drier than it is in New Mexico today, with rain falling only in certain seasons rather than year-round. By about 6,000 years ago, little grass grew in New Mexico, and the bison herds that used to roam there stayed farther north. The people of New Mexico adapted to this loss of bison meat by gathering more of their food from plants. They invented better techniques for preparing food and for hunting the few, small animals that remained to them, wringing as much nourishment as they could out of a very harsh environment. With that improved technology, when the climate became somewhat cooler and moister again, about 5,000 years ago, the people of New Mexico were able to feed themselves well enough to increase their population many times over, to perhaps 15,000 to 30,000 people. By 4,000 years ago, though, they had once again reached the limit of how many people they could feed–unless they could adapt yet again and find a new way of life that could allow more growth in population.

That new way of life would be agriculture.

Agriculture began in the Middle East about 11,000 years ago. This detail of a Mesopotamian clay seal showing cultivated grain dates back about 5,000 years.

chapter two

AGRICULTURE

All over the world, in different ways in different places, the dance between nature and culture played out as the great migration brought humans to nearly every place on Earth. Although human progress sometimes stalled or stagnated or even ran into a dead end, overall, the migration was a great success for humankind. Perhaps a few thousand of us lived in sub-Saharan Africa 60,000 years ago. By about 12,000 years ago, perhaps 5 million of us lived all over the world.

Much of that growth in population came after about 16,000 years ago, as Earth's climate warmed and glaciers retreated, leaving much more land free of ice and suitable for humans to live on. As the glaciers retreated, climate and growing conditions all over the world became more like what we see today. Meanwhile, here and there around the world, in places that favored it, groups of people figured out how to store food from seasonal

23

WORLD POPULATION

AGRICULTURE 5,000 BCE
about 10 million

PREHISTORY 10,000 BCE
about 5 million

times of plenty (when salmon come upstream to spawn, for example, or when whales or reindeer migrate close by) to eat all year or until the next seasonal bonanza.

One of these favored places was in the Middle East. There, about 15,000 years ago, bands of hunter-gatherers happened upon naturally occurring fields of wild barley

Over a period of thousands of years, agriculture was discovered independently in many places throughout the world.

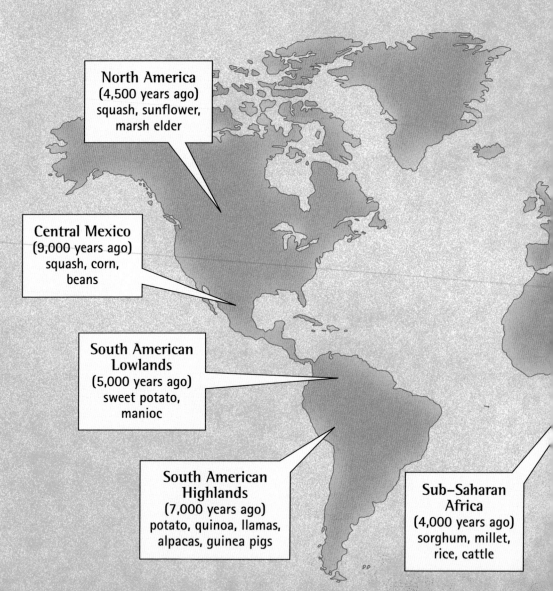

North America
(4,500 years ago)
squash, sunflower,
marsh elder

Central Mexico
(9,000 years ago)
squash, corn,
beans

South American Lowlands
(5,000 years ago)
sweet potato,
manioc

South American Highlands
(7,000 years ago)
potato, quinoa, llamas,
alpacas, guinea pigs

Sub-Saharan Africa
(4,000 years ago)
sorghum, millet,
rice, cattle

and wheat. On some hillsides, the barley and wheat grew in such abundance that harvesting them could provide enough food to last all year. The lucky people who found these fields no longer needed to roam far and wide in search of food. Settlements prospered near these fields for about 2,500 years. Then the climate changed slightly,

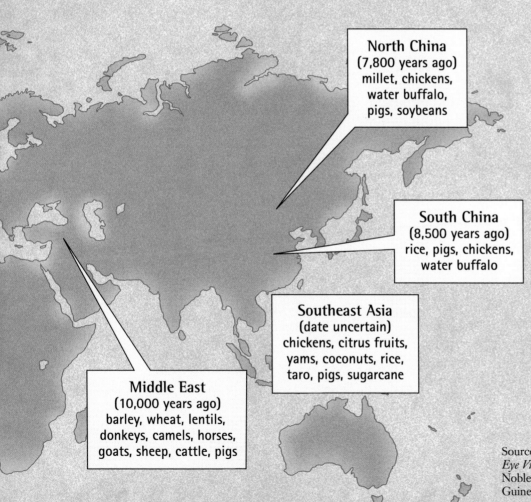

North China
(7,800 years ago)
millet, chickens,
water buffalo,
pigs, soybeans

South China
(8,500 years ago)
rice, pigs, chickens,
water buffalo

Southeast Asia
(date uncertain)
chickens, citrus fruits,
yams, coconuts, rice,
taro, pigs, sugarcane

Middle East
(10,000 years ago)
barley, wheat, lentils,
donkeys, camels, horses,
goats, sheep, cattle, pigs

Sources: J. R. McNeill and William McNeill, *The Human Web: A Bird's-Eye View of World History* (New York: W. W. Norton, 2003); John Noble Wilford, "An Early Heartland of Agriculture Is Found in New Guinea," *New York Times*, June 24, 2003.

becoming a bit drier. The wild barley and wheat began to die out. Eventually, in a few places, people began to plant seeds intentionally in especially wet places where the grains hadn't grown naturally before but could now, in the drier climate, grow well. In short, they took the first step toward becoming the world's first farmers.

By "farming" or "agriculture" we mean the intentional planting of food crops and tending of animals that over time become genetically distinct from their wild ancestors and dependent on humans for their survival—even as humans become dependent on eating them. Those first farmers in the Middle East show us how this works. Over time, the grains they planted were selected for qualities that suited farming. At first this happened without anyone understanding what was going on. Only grain that made it successfully through harvest and storage was planted the next year; only its genes were passed on to the next generation of plants. At some point, though, people began intentionally saving and planting only their best, fattest, easiest-to-grow grain. Generation by generation, the grain saved and grown by people became genetically different from its wild ancestors. The same thing happened with other food crops and soon with animals, too—first the wild ancestors of today's domesticated sheep and goats, and eventually cattle, pigs, donkeys, camels, and horses. Animals were selected for being tame and easy to handle; for superior meat, milk, wool, and fur; and ultimately for

Prehistoric Global Warming? For millions of years, Earth's levels of carbon dioxide and methane—"greenhouse" gases that allow heat from sunlight in but keep it from radiating off Earth into space—have risen and fallen in cycles thousands of years long. Both carbon dioxide and methane levels were at the high point of the cycle at the end of the most recent ice age, about 11,000 years ago, and began falling as they normally would. But just then, humans began farming. As growing numbers of farmers cut down more and more forest to plant fields, the amount of carbon dioxide in the air stopped falling and about 8,000 years ago began to rise—thousands of years ahead of when it normally would. Methane levels also stopped falling and began rising about 5,000 years ago, with the rise of irrigated rice farming in Asia. Together, these rising greenhouse gas levels headed off a new ice age that would have begun 4,000 or 5,000 years ago.

muscle power, to carry loads on their backs and pull carts and plows. (When people started farming with animals, they got more than they bargained for. Diseases that evolved with wild animals found new hosts in the humans who tended their domesticated descendants.) Between about 11,000 and 3,000 years ago, agriculture was discovered independently in at least half a dozen places all over the world. Everywhere it was adopted, agriculture put an end to roaming from place to place with a small group of people, hunting and gathering in season–the lifestyle that had carried humans all over Earth in their great migration out of Africa. Instead, agriculture demanded a lifestyle of settling in one place, a village, organized around the planting and tending and storage of food crops and the care and feeding of domesticated animals. In return for all the work of raising crops, agriculture offered such an advantage for people struggling to survive–a more reliable food supply–that it quickly spread from each place that discovered it.

In places where agriculture was adopted, the population grew quickly. This occurred in part because more food was produced (making it possible to feed more people) but also because farming not only allowed but actually required people to settle down and live in one place. The number of children a migrating hunter-gatherer could raise was limited by the need to carry infants from place to place. Until one child was old enough to walk, a mother couldn't carry around and care for any additional infants. Farming in one place eased that problem.

Farming, once adopted even partially, also tended to demand more and more reliance on it, with less reliance on traditional hunting and gathering. Farmers who needed to stay close to their fields to guard and tend them could no longer roam widely. A growing, settled population soon depleted game animals and other wild foods nearby.

Still, in some places, New Mexico for example, a dual way of life–some farming, some hunting and gathering–persisted for well over a thousand years. The farming of

28   corn spread from Central America north into New Mexico about 3,200 years ago. For hundreds of years, corn was planted each spring but tended very little through the growing season, leaving the people who planted it free to hunt and gather elsewhere before returning to harvest their corn in the fall. When bean farming was introduced, also from Central America, about 2,500 years ago, the people of New Mexico had all they needed to transform themselves into successful full-time farmers, except for one thing: a good enough reason to do so. As hunter-gatherers and casual farmers, they earned their living by working about five hundred hours each year. Full-time farmers of that time would have to work one thousand to two thousand hours each year. But then, also around 2,500 years ago, New Mexico's climate changed somewhat, so that rainfall was less reliable and predictable. Farming a surplus of food to store away for lean times began to look like a good idea, no matter how much work it took. When rainfall increased, several hundred years later, farmers were rewarded with more food, so most people in most places relied more and more on farming, less on hunting and gathering. The final straw that tipped the balance to nearly total reliance on farming was a new technology. Between 1,700 and 1,600 years ago, people in New Mexico learned how to make pottery, which allowed them to cook food with much less fuel and work. Combined with the development of varieties of corn with bigger ears (more food) and continued favorable weather, this spurred a sudden growth in population that could only be fed with farming. Too many people now lived in New Mexico to support themselves hunting and gathering.

> **Farming a surplus of food to store away for lean times began to look like a good idea, no matter how much work it took.**

Most historians believe corn was domesticated in the Tehuacán Valley of Mexico. The original wild form has long been extinct, but fossils dating back more than five thousand years indicate that early ears were small and the rows were irregular, much like the example at left.

All over the world, wherever agriculture was adopted, it eventually became the dominant way of life. With this shift came population growth unprecedented in human history. Our growing numbers spurred the next great milestone in human history: civilization.

Jerusalem was a teeming metropolis by the time of King Solomon's reign in the tenth century BCE.

chapter three

CRADLES OF CIVILIZATION

Civilization–first, foremost, everywhere, and every time–means cities, large numbers of people living clustered together and relying on farms outside the city for food. With cities come other features that together define what "civilization" means. Far-flung trade networks allow cities to get food from farmers and various other resources from all over to make into goods that can be traded for more food and resources. Cities, where people live permanently and in a highly organized pattern, allow for specialization of labor. That is, instead of everyone doing more or less the same kinds of work, one person might concentrate on being a skilled carpenter, another might be a priest, another a full-time

WORLD POPULATION		
CRADLES OF CIVILIZATION		
1000 BCE: 50 million		
1–1000 CE: 300 million		
AGRICULTURE 5,000 BCE		
about 10 million		
PREHISTORY 10,000 BCE		
about 5 million		

Writing Many people believe that the most important, defining achievement of civilization is writing, which allows us to reach across centuries into the mind of a stranger like nothing else can do. And in fact nearly every civilization has invented or adopted writing very early on. It's tempting to think that the inventors of writing must have been great poets or philosophers or at least storytellers, seeking to set down in writing words that would otherwise die with them. But it seems the earliest writing was actually done by accountants. People who needed to keep track of, say, how many goats changed hands in a business transaction, marked it down on clay. Other uses for writing, from recording laws to creating libraries, came later.

A receipt for five sheep from the Ur civilization, from around 2100 BCE.

soldier. This encourages the development of technology, as someone who works with weapons all day (for example) is more likely to think of improvements to or defenses against those weapons than someone who picks up a weapon only once in a while.

Cities and the wider civilization they establish also accumulate more wealth and distribute it more unequally than do either hunter-gatherers or small farming villages. Hunter-gatherers carry most of their wealth in the bone, muscle, and fat of their own bodies. Small farming villages beyond the reach of civilization aren't able to accumulate very much surplus wealth either, so if all of a village's people are to have enough to survive, none can have much more than the rest. Cities, though, can combine and amplify the accumulated wealth of many villages within reach of their civilization—enough wealth to allow survival of all, better conditions for some, and luxury for a few. Civilizations have enforced their unequal distributions of wealth in one or more of several ways.

Religion and knowledge. Religious leaders or wealthy people who support them have commanded wealth by promising to secure good weather or other blessings. In addition to acting as spiritual messengers, religious leaders in many early civilizations made careful observations of the Sun, stars, and seasons that enabled them to advise farmers when to plant crops, to warn sailors against storm seasons, and so on. Such valuable services can command a large share of wealth.

Commerce. Deal-makers in cities, where trade routes meet, can command great wealth by taking what's not so valuable in one place and bringing it to where it's more valuable. A farm village that isn't able to make its own metal tools will pay dearly for tools made in an urban workshop. Likewise, hungry city folks will pay more for food than what it costs back on the farm where it grows. Civilization links together distant, willing buyers and sellers. The deal-maker who delivers the right goods can become rich.

Force. Instead of making a deal, cities can send armies to distant places to take wealth by force. In the long run, armed force alone can't hold a civilization together. But in the short run, a superior military–better weapons, more or better-trained soldiers–can invade, conquer, and take what it wants. Better yet, a superior military can fight off such an invasion. Military protection is a valuable service, and those who provide it can command much wealth.

Just as farming enabled people to get more food and energy from nature than hunting and gathering did, so did civilization do a bigger and better job of this than village-based farming alone. Just as farming enabled a big increase in human population everywhere it was adopted, so did civilization enable a further increase. And just as hunter-gatherers spread out from Africa to every part of the world, and farmers and their way of life spread out from everywhere farming was adopted, so did civilization spread from each of its early centers.

Since civilization requires stable and productive farming to support it, it's no accident that the earliest civilizations sprang up in places where farming had been adopted early on.

Mesopotamia. Along and near the Tigris and Euphrates rivers, in present-day Iraq, the civilization of Sumer built a dozen or more cities beginning about 5,500 years ago. Sumer linked overseas and overland trade routes and used raw materials from afar to

34   make valuable trade goods such as woolen cloth, metal weapons, and tools. Sumerian goods and ideas spread far and wide through Europe and Asia—until the farmland that sustained Sumer's cities died, its soil poisoned with the slow buildup of salt from centuries of irrigation. Today the plains of Sumer are desert.

    India/Pakistan. Within a few hundred years after Sumer's cities were established, cities and civilization emerged along and near the Indus River and its tributaries. As with Sumer, trade and ideas from the Indus River cities reached far and wide. These cities were abandoned, though, about 3,500 years ago. We don't know for sure why. Raiders

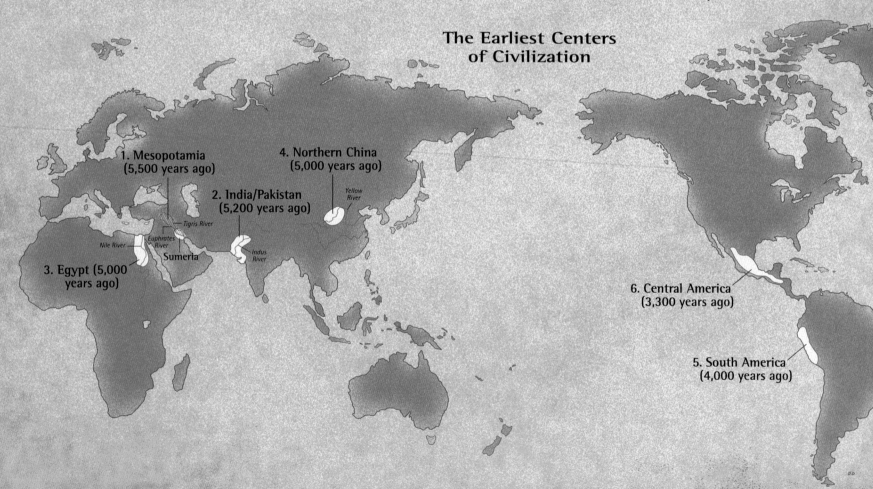

The Earliest Centers of Civilization

1. Mesopotamia (5,500 years ago)

4. Northern China (5,000 years ago)

2. India/Pakistan (5,200 years ago)

Yellow River

Tigris River

Euphrates River

Nile River

Sumeria

Indus River

3. Egypt (5,000 years ago)

6. Central America (3,300 years ago)

5. South America (4,000 years ago)

from the north, a people called Aryans, masters of the then-new style of warfare using horse-drawn chariots, ultimately took over the Indus River area and established their own civilization there.

Egypt. About five thousand years ago, the Nile River's exceptional usefulness for shipping and for watering farmland enabled the establishment of a stable and long-lived civilization along its riverbanks. The Nile's once-a-year floods brought water and a fresh layer of rich silt to the farmland—and flushed away harmful salts, which killed Sumer's soil. Egyptian civilization might well have continued for thousands of years longer if it hadn't been invaded and overrun by charioteers from Asia about 3,600 years ago.

Northern China. Large walled villages first appeared about five thousand years ago in the rich farmland atop cliffs near the midsection of the Huang He (Yellow) River. By about four thousand years ago, these towns were linked together under a common ruler, and their trade network stretched over much of Asia. About three thousand years ago, the foundation of Chinese civilization shifted from the clifftop plains to the floodplains of the river, as ambitious diking and drainage projects made the land there farmable.

South America. About four thousand years ago, cities and a distinctive civilization arose in the desert along the Pacific Coast of Peru. Rivers running down from the Andes Mountains were channeled for irrigation. Offshore currents brought good fishing close to shore, and access to diverse ecology—from ocean to desert to mountains—ensured a varied and reliable supply of food and other resources.

Central America. Quite separately from what was going on in South America, several successive civilizations

Fall of Civilizations With such good reasons why civilizations should do well, why and how do they eventually end? Some, like Chaco and Sumer, over-reach nature's capacity to support their way of life. Others, like Egypt, are conquered by invaders with superior weapons or better fighting techniques. Others, like Rome and China, are done in by disease—although worn-out natural resources and pressure from invaders also hurt. Once in a while, a natural catastrophe wipes out an entire civilization in one go. Minoan civilization, which came before Greek civilization on islands in the Mediterranean Sea around Crete, never recovered from an immense volcanic eruption in 1645 BCE.

36 arose in Central America, beginning with the Olmecs about 3,300 years ago. The Olmecs were organized and productive enough to build enormous mound structures and elaborate stone sculptures and to trade in precious goods from hundreds of miles away. The Olmecs' trade network may account for the spread of agriculture to New Mexico; the timing is right.

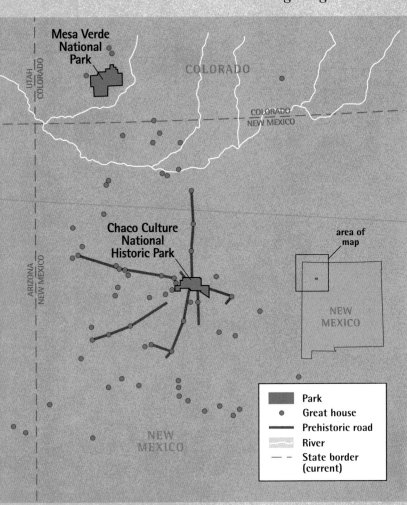

Mesa Verde
National
Park

UTAH
COLORADO

COLORADO

COLORADO
NEW MEXICO

ARIZONA
NEW MEXICO

Chaco Culture
National
Historic Park

area of
map

NEW
MEXICO

NEW
MEXICO

■ Park
● Great house
— Prehistoric road
〜 River
- - State border
(current)

While none of these early civilizations survive today, they didn't exactly "die," either. Trade networks sent each civilization's goods, ideas, and technology to faraway places, where often new cities and civilizations arose and grew strong and powerful—even as the cities and civilizations that got them started weakened and faded.

We can see this pattern in New Mexico. By 1,100 years ago, all of the good settlement and farming sites close to reliable springs in this region were already occupied near capacity. Small groups spread out over the land and planted scattered fields in the hope that the scattered, unreliable, sparse rainfall would hit enough of the fields to sustain all of the farmers. This strategy required both a vast increase in the amount of work done overall (for it assumed that many more fields would be planted each year than would yield a harvest) and an increase in trade. A regional peculiarity of climate conditions made Chaco Canyon in northwestern New Mexico a natural trade hub. To the west and north, precipitation typically fell in two seasons, winter and summer, whereas to the east and south, rainfall concentrated in July and August. And in fact, a trade system did develop so that when farmers in one climate zone had a surplus, it would be sent to granaries at Chaco in exchange for pottery, the chief currency of the day. When food was short, it would be bought with pottery.

So, at Chaco Canyon, beginning around 1,100 years ago and continuing for two centuries, the multistoried great houses whose ruins we can see today were built. Ultimately more than a million square feet of floor space for residences, ritual, and food

Pueblo Bonito, or "pretty village" in Spanish, is the largest and most famous ruin in Chaco Canyon. At its prime, Pueblo Bonito reached five stories in height along its back wall and may have contained as many as eight hundred rooms.

38 storage were enclosed here, under roofs held up by nearly a quarter of a million ponderosa pine trunks carried in from forests as far as 60 miles away, all at the cost of millions of hours of labor. Chaco was the center of civilization—of religion, knowledge, and social order as well as trade—for one hundred smaller towns and as many as 20,000 farm villages spread out over some 40,000 square miles. As such, Chaco and the elite who lived there commanded more and more food and labor and other resources as the civilization expanded and the population grew. This could work well only as long as surpluses remained available.

But by nine hundred years ago, much of the outlying farmland and wild lands on which Chaco relied had become degraded. Soil fertility was drained, wood and wild food supplies were depleted. That Chacoan civilization was living beyond the land's carrying capacity can be read in the overworked, undernourished skeletons of people who lived there then. But not all Chacoans suffered equally. Burial sites tell us that malnutrition and the number of children who died were much worse in the farming villages than among the elite at Chaco, especially but not exclusively in times of drought.

Compare this evidence with the dates of construction work at Chaco and on its extensive road system, and it's obvious that the Chaco response to hard times was not to pull back and restrict population, nor to create new technology to improve efficiency or expand the food supply. Instead they funneled labor into bigger and bigger public works projects, from huge buildings to far-flung roads. When a decade of drought came—a drought the hunter-gatherer ancestors of the Chacoans could easily have survived, with their more flexible and sustainable way of life intact—the farmers whose work had built and sustained Chaco abandoned it. The city of

> **Chaco was the center of civilization—of religion, knowledge, and social order as well as trade—for one hundred smaller towns and as many as 20,000 farm villages spread out over some 40,000 square miles.**

Chaco Canyon, no longer sustained by the belief that its trade and ritual and power could ensure prosperity, emptied and fell into ruin.

But even though all that remains of the city of Chaco is ruins, Chaco's civilization didn't completely die. Long after the collapse of Chaco, outposts of civilization derived from Chaco flourished in the region. The best known of these is the spectacular community of cliff dwellings at Mesa Verde, in southwestern Colorado, now also in ruins. And even today we can see living traces of Chaco in the Pueblo peoples of New Mexico,

Ancestral Puebloans occupied what is now Mesa Verde in Colorado from approximately CE 1 to CE 1300. The thousands of known archaeological sites at Mesa Verde include hundreds of cliff dwellings.

Led by King Attila, the Huns attacked many parts of the Roman Empire during the 430s and 440s CE. Unable to win decisive victories, they were eventually absorbed into the peoples of southeastern Europe.

chapter four
AGE OF EMPIRES

For thousands of years, a familiar pattern prevailed. In places all over the world where farming was successful, the population grew. Then, either independently or stimulated by ideas and goods from distant cities, new cities and civilizations arose, and population grew further. People and ideas and trade goods spread out from each center of civilization. When for one reason or another a center of civilization declined, its ideas and technology and goods were already out there, spread far and wide and available for use by later centers of civilization.

Of these networks of civilization, the one that became most powerful and far-reaching stretched across time and space from Greece to Rome to Europe. Greek civilization arose about 2,800 years ago (800 BCE) in the great sweep of land where farming had spread from its first homeland in the Middle East. Greece inherited ideas

41

WORLD POPULATION

AGE OF EMPIRES
1200–1400 CE: 400 million
1500 CE: 500 million
1750 CE: 790 million
1800 CE: 980 million

CRADLES OF CIVILIZATION
1000 BCE: 50 million
1–1000 CE: 300 million

AGRICULTURE 5,000 BCE
about 10 million

PREHISTORY 10,000 BCE
about 5 million

42 and technology and ways of life from the earliest civilizations (Sumer, Egypt, and India/Pakistan) and from their successors around and near the Mediterranean Sea.

The Greek way of civilization was successful enough that hundreds of its cities were established around the Mediterranean, tied together through trade and common religion, language, and culture. The achievements of Greek art, literature, architecture, philosophy, and science were so great that when the Greek city-states were finally conquered, their Macedonian conquerors adopted Greek civilization wholesale. Alexander the Great (son of the conquering King Philip of Macedonia) spread elements of Greek civilization as far as India. After Alexander died, his empire fell apart. But Greek civilization persisted.

About 2,200 years ago (215–146 BCE), the rising civilization of Rome conquered Greece. But in a way, Greece conquered the Romans, who absorbed much of Greek civilization into their own and spread it farther than any empire had ever reached before. Roman civilization built on and added to the achievements of the Greeks. It also spread the new religion of Christianity throughout its empire, beginning shortly after Jesus' crucifixion, about 30 CE. Within that empire, Roman law enabled various peoples to live together under a common set of rules. Because Roman law made it reasonably safe to travel throughout the entire vast region ruled by it, migration and trade flourished. People from all over Europe and the Mediterranean mingled, exchanging not only trade goods but also ideas and information from different places and ways of life. This sharing and spreading of knowledge made possible countless improvements in technology—and also made it much less likely that innovation and knowledge would be lost forever if catastrophe befell the one and only place where people knew about it.

Alexander the Great, king of Macedonia, conquered the Persian Empire, which stretched from the Mediterranean Sea to India. He also spread Greek ideas and customs in Egypt and western Asia.

In less than a thousand years, the hugely successful run of Greek and Roman civilization brought a tremendous population boom. By two thousand years ago, the population of the Roman Empire was perhaps 60 million—likely more than the population of the entire world just a thousand years earlier.

But this boom brought with it the seeds of its own destruction. So many people crowding the land stripped forests of their trees and soil of its fertility. Erosion of soil from Greek hillsides and a general decline in the quality of its farmlands weakened the Greek city-states and contributed to their downfall. Rome to some extent outran this depletion of natural resources by conquering distant lands. But that solution brought with it problems of its own. As Rome's empire grew, it became more and more difficult

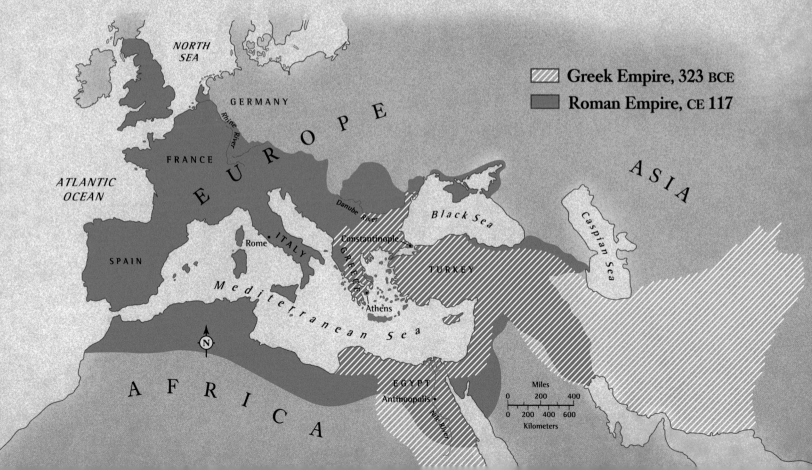

Greek Empire, 323 BCE
Roman Empire, CE 117

NORTH SEA

GERMANY

Rhine River

EUROPE

FRANCE

ATLANTIC OCEAN

Danube River

ASIA

Black Sea

Caspian Sea

ITALY

Rome

Constantinople

GREECE

TURKEY

SPAIN

Mediterranean Sea

Athens

N

EGYPT

Antinoopolis

Nile River

AFRICA

Miles
0   200   400

0   200   400   600
Kilometers

44 to govern its increasingly faraway and foreign peoples. In places where it had once seemed that Rome offered a pretty good deal (some wealth sent to Rome in return for order and increased trade), people began to question whether they wouldn't be better off on their own. Holding on to its territory by paying off or putting down disgruntled natives became more and more expensive for Rome.

Rome couldn't outrun another hazard of its population boom: disease. People crowded together in dirty cities bred epidemics. Worse still, the human population at that time had not yet been exposed to the diseases of domesticated animals consistently enough to have developed much immunity. Such diseases could and did rip through cities with devastating effects. Between 165 and 180 CE, epidemics killed enough people to reduce the population of the Roman Empire by about a quarter. (In China, much the

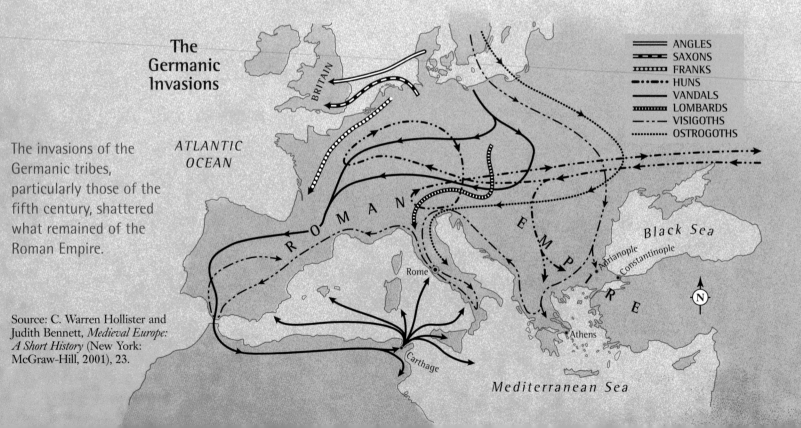

The invasions of the Germanic tribes, particularly those of the fifth century, shattered what remained of the Roman Empire.

Source: C. Warren Hollister and Judith Bennett, *Medieval Europe: A Short History* (New York: McGraw-Hill, 2001), 23.

same thing happened at about the same time, killing a quarter of its empire of perhaps 60 million people.) The Roman Empire never recovered and gradually collapsed.

No successor immediately took up where the Roman Empire left off. For hundreds of years, German and other "barbarian"(as the Romans called them) invaders swirled through Europe, followed a few hundred years later by Vikings from the north, Hungarians from the east, and Saracens from the south. Beset by waves of war and disease, civilization in Europe stalled. Then, in the 1300s, the Black Death (an epidemic of a form of bubonic plague) combined with other hardships to kill off perhaps one-third of Europe's people. Elsewhere in the world, though, civilizations from the Americas to India to the Middle East did well enough that world population overall held roughly steady at about 300 million for close to a thousand years. About 1200 CE it bumped upward toward 400 million, where (Black Death notwithstanding) it remained in 1400 CE.

Meanwhile, Roman civilization and the Greek civilization it had absorbed weren't completely lost. For more than a thousand years, some of the knowledge accumulated by Greece and Rome was conserved in the monasteries of the Christian religion Rome had spread through Europe. After 634 CE, the scholars of Islam collected and preserved even more of this knowledge in their centers of learning around the Mediterranean and Middle East. They added to it knowledge gathered from India as well as Muslim scholars' own contributions to science and mathematics. When, in the 1400s, thinkers

During the eighth through tenth centuries, various invaders further altered the political and cultural face of Europe.

The Viking, Hungarian, and Saracen Invasions

VIKINGS

——— VIKINGS
------ HUNGARIANS
- - - SARACENS

ATLANTIC OCEAN

ICELAND

SCOTLAND

IRELAND

ENGLAND

NORWAY

SWEDEN

DENMARK

HUNGARIANS

N

CORSICA

SARDINIA

BALEARIC I.

SICILY

SARACENS

Mediterranean Sea

Source: C. Warren Hollister and Judith Bennett, *Medieval Europe: A Short History* (New York: McGraw-Hill, 2001), 105.

First Humans to Sail around the World

In 1519 an expedition of five ships headed by the Portuguese adventurer Ferdinand Magellan set sail from Spain, aiming to be the first to circumnavigate Earth. Their biggest surprise along the way was the size of the Pacific Ocean, which Magellan expected to cross in a few weeks. It actually took more than three months—with not nearly enough food and water on board for such a long time at sea. One of the men on board describes what this was like:

"We were three months and twenty days without getting any kind of fresh food. We ate biscuit, which was no longer biscuit, but powder of biscuits swarming with worms, for they had eaten the good. It stank strongly of the urine of rats. We drank yellow water that had been putrid for many days. We also ate some ox hides that covered the top of the mainyard . . . . Rats were sold for one-half ducado [about $1.16 in gold] apiece. . . . The gums of both the lower and the upper teeth of some of our men swelled, so that they could not eat under any circumstances and therefore died. Nineteen men died from that sickness."

Nearly three years after it set out, the expedition's one surviving ship returned home. Of the original crew of about 250 men, only 18 survived. Magellan himself was among those who died.

Antonio Pigafetta, *Magellan's Voyage: A Narrative of the First Circumnavigation*, edited by R. A. Skelton (Mineola, NY: Dover Publications, 1994), 57.

and doers in the Mediterranean region combined the knowledge stored up by both Christendom and Islam, the stage was set for yet another leap ahead in human migration and population—the first civilization with worldwide reach.

Six hundred years ago, about 1400 CE, humans lived nearly everywhere on Earth, but no one living at that time knew it. Even the most powerful and sophisticated of the world's civilizations, in Europe and Asia, had little contact with or knowledge of other peoples in Europe, Asia, and Africa. They knew nothing at all of the Americas or Australia. That would soon change.

In the 1400s, savvy shipbuilders put together knowledge from the Mediterranean region, western Europe, and the Baltic Sea and developed new designs for ships and sails better able to go farther and faster, carrying more people and cargo. At the same time, the hands-on knowledge of Mediterranean sailors combined with the math and science of Muslim scholars in the region to vastly improve navigation. This made it much more likely that people sailing farther and farther away on those new ships would be able to return home safely.

Beginning in the 1430s, sailors from Portugal ventured farther and farther down the west coast of Africa, and they returned home to prove it could be done. At first, the Portuguese were seeking gold from parts of Africa's interior previously unexplored by Europeans. Later, after the pioneering sailor Vasco da Gama made it beyond Africa's southern tip in 1497, the Portuguese sailed to and from India and southern China, reaping vast profits on spices and silks that could be bought cheaply in the Far East and sold for a fortune in Europe.

The Portuguese in the 1400s were basically sailing around the perimeter of the world then known to Europeans. Christopher Columbus, working for neighboring Spain, tried something completely different—sailing boldly out to sea, west from Europe into uncharted ocean, expecting to reach Asia by a route no one knew was sailable. And in fact, it wasn't. Although Columbus at first mistook the Caribbean islands he found in 1492 for unknown islands off the east coast of Asia, all Europe soon realized that Columbus had instead found islands off a vast and previously unknown land between Europe and Asia. That land was the Americas.

By the early 1500s, Spain, Portugal, and other European powers were furiously competing for new lands and trading ventures in the Americas as well as in Africa and Asia. Wherever they went, Europeans brought back not only trade goods but also knowledge, from new observations of nature to new edible and useful plants. This fresh knowledge further

Vasco da Gama's voyage to India in 1498 opened a new trade route between Europe and Asia. He is shown here at the Court of Zamorin of Calicut, India.

stimulated science in Europe, which in turn improved Europeans' power to travel, trade, and conquer. Such an expansion of science and commerce had never before been seen. Within three hundred years, Spanish, Portuguese, English, French, and Dutch explorers, traders, conquerors, and missionaries laid claim to most of the inhabited world considered "uncivilized" by Europeans–the Americas, Africa, Australia, and much of Asia and the Pacific islands.

Europe's empires were not created equal. Spain and Portugal (by the late 1500s, they were ruled by one king) had the advantage of a head start in long-distance exploration by sea. They used this advantage in the 1500s to secure I-got-here-first rights to much of the world previously unknown to Europeans. Their main aim was to ship as much gold back home as possible. The Dutch and the British took a different path, seeking not just treasure but long-term trade–even if they had to plant their own people in faraway places to grow or develop goods to be traded. This model for empire proved much more successful, especially for Great Britain. By the end of the 1700s, the British Empire circled the globe.

The Dutch and British model for empire created prosperity unknown in previous human history. Until about 1700, wherever and whenever humans prospered, population soon increased as fast as wealth did, so that the average wealth per person stayed about the same. But beginning in the late 1600s, the Dutch and British managed to increase both their population and the average wealth per person, so that most people lived at least as well as their parents had and

Columbus's historic voyage to the "New World" was the beginning of contact between Europe and the Western Hemisphere.

some people lived far more luxuriously indeed. They did this by sending large numbers of people to live in faraway parts of the world where valuable resources could be exploited and extracted for the benefit of both the European emigrants and their home countries. The British record of migration during this time is mind-boggling: Between about 1600 and 1950, some 20 million people left Britain–more than twice the entire population of England and Wales in 1800.

The expansion of European empires all over the world brought great transformations of landscapes and vast migrations of people–and death and destruction.

The Spanish Empire reached its territorial peak in the early 1790s. The British Empire was at its largest and most powerful around 1920, when more than one-quarter of the world's land and one-quarter of its population was claimed by Britain.

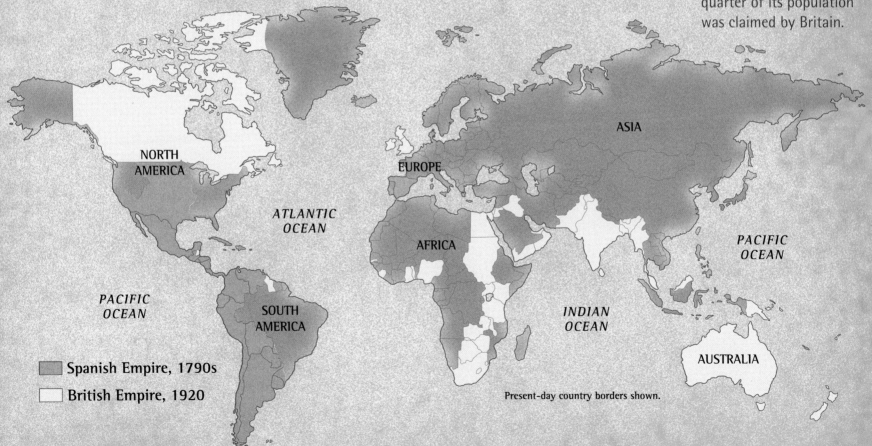

Spanish Empire, 1790s

British Empire, 1920

Present-day country borders shown.

50   The specific effects of Europeans meeting non-Europeans were different in different places. In Africa, for example, slavery had long been a local practice. Europeans turned it into a big transcontinental business, perhaps ten times as large as it had been when it was confined to Africa. What drove this business was European demand for labor in the Americas to grow sugar, tobacco, cotton, and coffee–high-value crops that required a lot of work to plant, tend, harvest, and prepare for market. Altogether, between 11 and 14 million Africans were sold as slaves in markets along the African coast and sent to the Americas.

Zheng He Between 1405 and 1433, the Chinese admiral Zheng He led six ocean-going expeditions that dwarfed Christopher Columbus's nearly a century later. On the 1414 expedition alone, Zheng He took along perhaps 30,000 people on dozens of ships much larger than Columbus's. Their explorations took them five thousand to six thousand miles from home. Then the Chinese government decided to turn its back on long-distance seafaring trade and exploration. Zheng He's great ships rotted in harbor. A generation later, the knowledge needed to build them was lost from China, not to be recovered for hundreds of years.

In the Americas, at least half and perhaps as much as 90 percent of the native population succumbed to epidemics of European diseases in the 150 years after Columbus's first arrival in 1492. (Few animals suitable for use in agriculture are native to the Americas. Lack of domesticated animals both slowed the development of civilization there and ensured that Native Americans would have no immunity to the diseases that originated in domesticated animals in Europe.) Then, beginning in the 1620s, large numbers of Europeans migrated to the Americas, so that by 1800, the total number of people living in America had risen again to near what it was before Columbus.

Overall, despite the death and destruction Europeans brought to non-European peoples, the population of the world grew to an all-time high between 1500 and 1800, roughly doubling to perhaps 900 million people. In large part, this was due to the spread, via European trade routes, of food crops that used to be grown only in one region to places all over the world, increasing the quantity and variety of food wherever they could

be grown. The most important of these were maize (American corn), cassava (manioc), and potatoes, which spread from their original home in the Americas to Europe, Africa, Asia, and the Pacific. Another reason for the world's population growth was a change in the way humans experienced the various diseases originally given to them by livestock thousands of years ago. First-time exposure to these diseases brought catastrophic epidemics to native peoples in the Americas, Australia, the Pacific, and parts of Africa. But the great increase in travel and migration after 1500 meant that all places were exposed to all of these diseases all the time. As in Europe and other places where these same diseases had long come as occasional epidemics, people developed immunity, fewer died, and by the 1700s, population was increasing nearly everywhere in the world, even in the places hardest hit by the catastrophic epidemics of the 1500s and 1600s.

A nineteenth-century slave market shows native Africans being readied to ship to the Americas. From the 1500s to the 1800s, Europeans shipped between 11 and 14 million slaves to the Western Hemisphere. The majority went to the sugar colonies in South and Central America, mainly Brazil. About 6 percent went to North America.

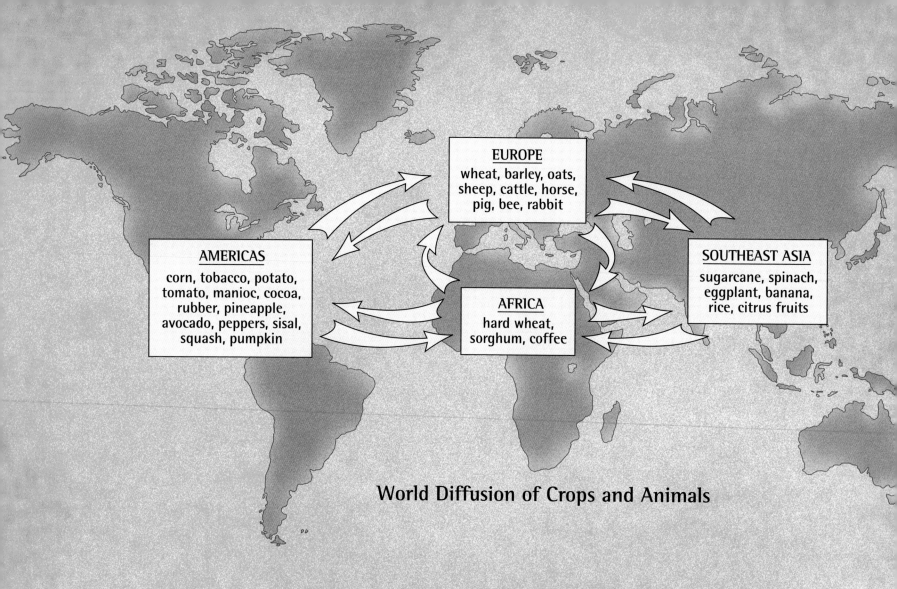

EUROPE
wheat, barley, oats,
sheep, cattle, horse,
pig, bee, rabbit

AMERICAS
corn, tobacco, potato,
tomato, manioc, cocoa,
rubber, pineapple,
avocado, peppers, sisal,
squash, pumpkin

AFRICA
hard wheat,
sorghum, coffee

SOUTHEAST ASIA
sugarcane, spinach,
eggplant, banana,
rice, citrus fruits

World Diffusion of Crops and Animals

By 1800 western European nations, Russia, and the descendants of Europeans in the United States controlled about one-third of the world. By 1878 they controlled two-thirds. European empire building continued around the world into the beginning of the twentieth century, when China's resistance to outside influence collapsed under pressure from Europeans eager to do business in Asia.

But even as Europe's empires were growing in some parts of the world, they were crumbling elsewhere, much like the Roman Empire did centuries earlier. Beginning with the American Revolution in the 1770s, parts of the world controlled by Europe began to resent sending wealth to Europe, began to want to govern themselves, and began to break away from European rule. A crescendo of unraveling in the twentieth century left only token bits of European empires remaining by the mid-1960s.

Still, Europeans and European-Americans prospered. Their standard of living and population didn't falter but grew tremendously in the 1800s and 1900s. What supported this growth was energy.

Oregon Trail Millions of European-Americans migrated west in the 1800s from the eastern part of the United States. One of the most popular routes was the Oregon Trail from Missouri to the Pacific Coast. Perhaps a quarter-million people traveled the Oregon Trail during the years it was used most, from the early 1840s to the early 1850s. Their average speed, on horseback or in wagons or on foot, was just three miles an hour. Getting from Missouri to California or Oregon could take more than four months. Along the way, many died of disease, thirst, hunger, accidents, and frostbite. The trail fell into disuse as railroads took its place.

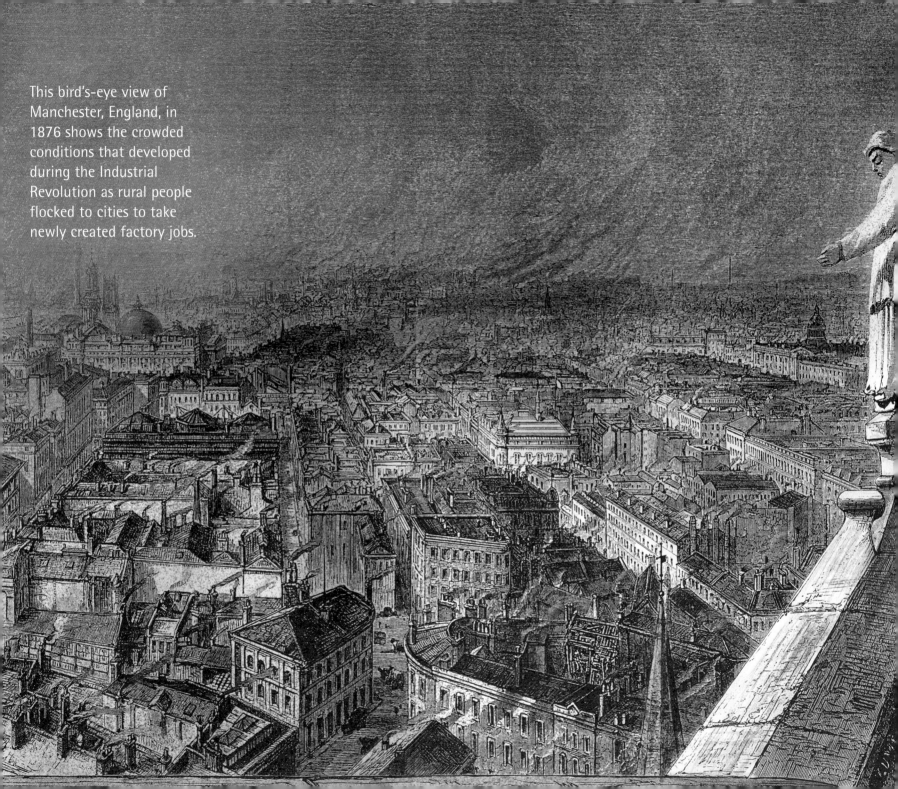

This bird's-eye view of Manchester, England, in 1876 shows the crowded conditions that developed during the Industrial Revolution as rural people flocked to cities to take newly created factory jobs.

chapter five

AGE OF ENERGY

In 1800 most of the world's people lived much as they had in the thousands of years since humans first became farmers. Most people still made their living farming, and farms were still run on the muscle power of humans and animals, fueled by sunlight of the past year or so stored as food, with only a little help from wind or water power in places that favored it. Fuel for heating and cooking came from trees. Most goods were produced and consumed locally, not shipped to or from afar. People knew exactly where and by whom most of what they ate and wore and used was produced, and nearly everyone was either self-employed or worked for someone they personally knew, who lived nearby. Very few people–maybe 2 percent of the world's population–lived in cities.

      Then, in just a few decades, everything changed. The harnessing of millions of years worth of stored solar energy (in the form of coal, mostly, at first) combined with a

55

WORLD POPULATION

AGE OF ENERGY
1850 CE: 1,260 million
1900 CE: 1,650 million
1950 CE: 2,520 million
2000 CE: 6 billion

AGE OF EMPIRES
1200–1400 CE: 400 million
1500 CE: 500 million
1750 CE: 790 million
1800 CE: 980 million

CRADLES OF CIVILIZATION
1000 BCE: 50 million
1–1000 CE: 300 million

AGRICULTURE 5,000 BCE
about 10 million

PREHISTORY 10,000 BCE
about 5 million

By the mid-1800s, factories were using vast amounts of coal to power machinery. This scene shows power textile looms in Great Britain.

cluster of technological advances in an explosion of activity known to history as the Industrial Revolution. Europe ran short of wood for fuel and began turning to coal as early as the 1500s and extensively by the 1700s, as the Industrial Revolution took off in England. The United States depended largely on wood fuel and water power for energy until the 1880s, then shifted to coal as Europe had done. Coal-powered steam engines powered the mining of much more coal, which powered many more engines. The engines were set to doing more and more kinds of work, from pushing boats upstream to running railroads, factories, and more.

Because Europe industrialized before anyplace else, Europeans and their American descendants in the 1800s and early 1900s grew faster than all other peoples in number, wealth, and power. They took what they needed to do so from around the world along the way, transforming landscapes in ways unimaginable without the power of fossil fuels and the powerful machines that rely on them.

This can perhaps best be seen in the United States. There, a fast-growing population swelled by millions of migrants from Europe seized vast quantities of natural resources and shipped them off to distant markets. As resources were mined out of one

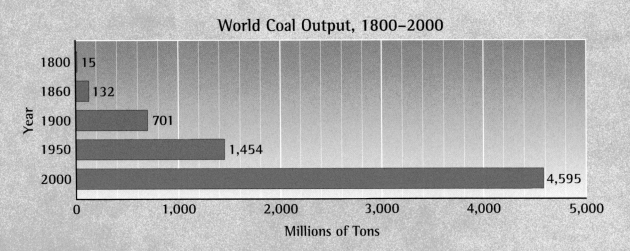

World Coal Output, 1800–2000

Year	Millions of Tons
1800	15
1860	132
1900	701
1950	1,454
2000	4,595

Coal-burning steam engines were the main source of power for industry in the 1800s. Since then, while coal burning has increased hugely, so has the use of other kinds of energy. Coal provides less than one-quarter of the world's energy today.

place, the market moved on to another, then another. For example, after the great forests of the eastern United States were cut down, the northern forests of Minnesota, Wisconsin, and Michigan were cut to supply lumber for the farmers and ranchers setting themselves up on America's treeless prairie west of the Mississippi River in the latter half of the 1800s. As prairie farming took off, the flood of cheap beef and grain it sent to market back east drove New England's farmers out of business. (New England's hilly landscape was not well suited for mass production of such crops, and hard use had already used up much of its soil fertility.) Some of New England's farmers moved west to fresher fields; more moved to booming northeastern factory towns. There cotton from the faraway south and other raw materials were manufactured into great quantities of finished goods that were then shipped back to the south and off to the west, where farmers and ranchers produced even greater quantities of foodstuffs to ship back east to feed the factory workers. As America's production and consumption grew, so did its population—explosively, from about 5 million in 1800 to more than 76 million in 1900.

Before the conservation movement began in the United States in the 1890s, wasteful land use destroyed large areas of forest.

The great growth in wealth unleashed by the fossil-fueled Industrial Revolution made such growth in population possible, and not just in the United States. In the two centuries of the Age of Energy, 1800 to 2000, the world had to feed five times as many people as it did in 1800. To do this, vast amounts of grassland and forest were turned into farmland. But the land available for this in 1800 wasn't where the people were. Europe and much of Asia had long before then turned into farmland nearly every scrap of land where food could grow. Most of the new farmland of the mid-1800s to mid-1900s was found in North America and to a lesser extent in the black-soil regions of Russian territory and in Australia and Latin America. Large numbers of people migrated to these places to farm, and the food they grew fed ever-larger numbers of people elsewhere. At the same time, much land in parts of Africa and Asia was converted from farmland that fed local peoples to farmland growing cash crops for export. None of this would have been possible without the mining of fossil fuels to power transportation.

The population explosion of the nineteenth and twentieth centuries was made possible not just by more food but also by less death. More babies made it through childhood to become adults, and adults lived longer, too. There were several reasons for this. More food meant better nutrition, leading to better health. At the same time, advances in the scientific understanding of disease led to better ways to prevent diseases that used to weaken or kill many people. Public supplies of clean drinking water and effective sewage systems, for example, vastly improved the health of European and American cities beginning in the 1800s, when the population explosion in the more developed, more industrialized parts of the world took off.

People in every place touched by the Industrial Revolution—ultimately, everywhere in the world—migrated from the countryside to the rapidly growing industrial centers of Europe and America. This migration accelerated in the twentieth century as industry developed further and as the usefulness of petroleum came to be exploited fully. In America, for example, in 1920 one-fourth of all farmland was still devoted to feeding working farm animals. Soon

Death of Languages As previously isolated peoples around the world have become more and more in touch with one another, their languages have been dying. The people who used to speak them now speak English or other languages in common use around the world or in their region, to communicate with people they didn't need to know in the past. Still, in the twenty-first century, more than six thousand languages are spoken around the world. About one-sixth of those languages are spoken by only fifty or fewer groups of people, though. Linguists estimate that half of today's languages will be dead, or no longer spoken, within the next century.

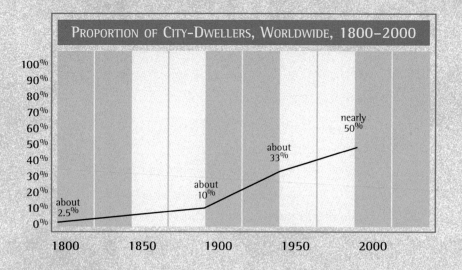

PROPORTION OF CITY-DWELLERS, WORLDWIDE, 1800–2000

thereafter, petroleum-powered machinery replaced the plow horse and replaced more and more farmworkers as well. Farmers of cotton and wheat and other such commodities (products the marketplace treats the same no matter where or how they're produced) found that those who didn't have the money to buy expensive machinery and big farms to run it on couldn't stay in business. Industrial agriculture produced more and more food with fewer farmers to feed more townfolk. Millions of people left America's countryside and moved to America's larger towns, cities, and suburbs, to live lives their great-grandparents couldn't have imagined. Rural places all over the country emptied out. As cities and the industry in them grew, they became crowded and dirty. Eventually, while poorer workers still migrated to live and work in city centers, wealthier people began instead to migrate to live in suburbs while still working in the city centers. This pattern began to be seen in Europe and America in the mid-1800s, as new public railway systems made daily commutes from suburbs to city centers much easier.

The changes for America's countryside and for the remaining people working it 61
sped up after World War II (1939–1945). Investment in expensive, specialized
equipment both demanded and rewarded bigger and more uniform fields and farms.
Native plants and animals were squeezed out. Vast fields planted intensively with one
crop both sucked nutrients out of the soil and invited problems with insects and other
pests, all of which demanded and rewarded a cascade of technological fixes. The
petrochemical industry devised new herbicides, pesticides, and fertilizers. Plant breeders
devised new, high-yielding, hybrid varieties of seed for corn, wheat, and other food
crops that would thrive in this new farming system. These genetically identical seeds
would grow uniformly, would tolerate machine handling, chemicals, and irrigation, and
would produce huge crops given the right combination of inputs. In 1930 virtually none
of America's cornfields, for example, was planted with these proprietary hybrids; by
1970 virtually all were.

From the beginning of the Industrial Revolution in Europe and the United States,
other parts of the world–most of Africa, Latin America, and Asia–lagged behind. Much as

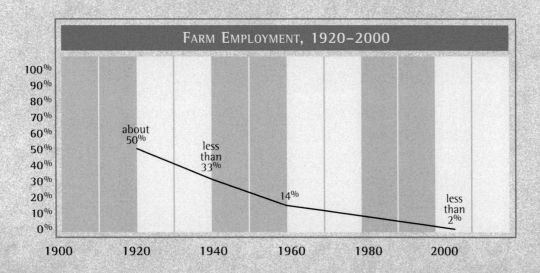

European cities suffered the same overcrowded conditions as American urban areas, as evidenced by this Victorian print of a London neighborhood in the mid-1800s.

the U.S. economy exploited the untapped resources of America (and other places, too) in the 1800s, so did European economies exploit untapped resources from around the world. Less-developed places remained less-developed well into the twentieth century, providing raw materials for European and American factories but having little industry of their own.

As Europe and America industrialized, the use-it-up-and-move-on pattern seen in America also played out in the wider world, with much of the less-industrialized parts of the world supplying raw materials for industry in the United States and especially

Europe. When one such source became depleted or more expensive or too much encumbered with pollution or other ill effects, industry abandoned it and moved on to fresh supplies elsewhere. At the same time, the pattern seen in the United States of using farmland for cash crops for distant markets, rather than for crops to feed people locally, also played out in the wider world. Less-developed countries were increasingly at the mercy of distant industries and markets over which they had no influence. Both of these patterns combined with cheaper, easier, fossil-fueled transportation to stimulate migration of fortune-seekers to distant countries, chiefly the United States, which offered economic opportunities not available in less-developed parts of the world. These worldwide economic patterns persisted even as European political control of less-developed countries unraveled in the first half of the twentieth century.

In the second half of the twentieth century, less-developed countries all over the world aimed to follow the European-American example of industrial development. But because places like Japan, Brazil, and China could learn from the European-American experience and begin their industrialization with much more advanced technology, their industrialization proceeded much, much faster.

And so did population growth, even in the least developed parts of the world. Between 1950 and 2000, the population of the world overall more than doubled, from 2.5 billion to 6 billion. By far, most of that increase was in the less-developed countries of the world, where population nearly tripled.

To feed the world's growing population, industrial agriculture increased its output, and still more land was converted to farmland. By 1950, though, most of the land suitable for farming in parts of the world with temperate climates was already being farmed. Since then, most of the land converted to farming has been in the tropics, particularly in tropical rain forests. (Scientists believe that AIDS is one result of people migrating into and altering tropical forests where few people used to be. The virus that

64 causes AIDS probably jumped from chimpanzees to humans who killed them in central Africa in the 1950s, perhaps earlier.) But the gains from this most recent conversion to farmland have been limited, for the soils of the tropics are typically much less rich than those of farmland in temperate zones. At the same time, the increasingly global industrial system of growing and marketing food has become even more dependent on the mining of fossil fuels for transport and refrigeration and increasingly to power irrigation and supply fertilizers and other chemical inputs.

Since 1950 industrial agriculture has vastly increased the world's production of food. There's now more than enough to feed all of the world's vastly increased population—if the food were distributed to all in need. Industrial agriculture has also further enabled the world's rich to get richer, while the poor have tended to remain poor. Much like commodity farmers in the United States, in less-developed countries, only those farmers who can afford to buy expensive specialized seed and the fertilizers and pesticides it requires for good yield will prosper. Others will likely fail and join the migration from countryside to city, leaving behind larger farms with fewer farmers. Many will seek to join the millions who have migrated in recent decades to countries with better economic opportunities—the United States, Canada, Australia, European nations, and the oil-rich countries of the Middle East.

Migrating Diseases Global warming and globalization of the world's economy are literally making us sick. AIDS, SARS, West Nile virus, dengue fever, and many more diseases have spread to parts of the world far from where they first emerged, carried by human or other hosts. In the cases of West Nile and dengue, warmer weather has allowed disease-carrying mosquitoes brought to faraway places to thrive where they would have struggled or died in colder times.

Many more will end up in the rapidly growing cities of the less-developed parts of the world. Overall, in both more-developed and less-developed parts of the world, urbanization (the concentration of people in cities) accelerated in the second half of the twentieth century. Population experts project that in 2007, for the first time in human history, more people will live in cities than in the countryside.

Population growth in the less-developed parts of the world has been enabled not only by more food but also by the belated arrival of the kinds of public health measures (clean water, sewer systems) that helped enable rapid population growth in the more-developed parts of the world nearly a century earlier. These measures spread to many less-developed parts of the world between 1945 and 1965–just in time to accompany new vaccines, antibiotics, and other measures that fended off death and improved health further still. Altogether, this meant that the population explosion of the less-developed world in the late twentieth century was hugely bigger than the earlier European-American population explosion.

Meanwhile, in the more-developed parts of the world–with Europe once again in the lead, beginning early in the twentieth century–population growth has slowed down. The prosperity that comes with industrialization at first enables larger families to survive and sustain themselves. But before long, family size in industrialized countries begins to shrink, not because people are starving to death but because more and more people choose to have fewer children. There are several reasons for this. For families now making a living from industry rather than farming, small children are more of an economic burden than a benefit. Meanwhile, as prosperity improves life expectancy, it

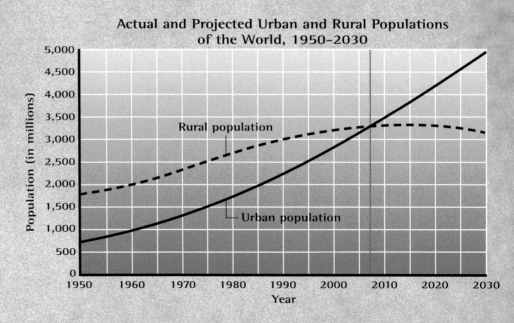

Actual and Projected Urban and Rural Populations of the World, 1950–2030

Source: United Nations Department of Economic and Social Affairs/Population Division, *World Urbanization Prospects: The 2003 Revision* (New York: United Nations, 2004), 4.

66 becomes reasonable to believe that even a small family will see some of its children survive to adulthood. (In most preindustrial societies, people expected half or more of their children to die young.)

So, population growth slowed in more-developed countries in the first half of the twentieth century, but it didn't stop. And the population of cities in more-developed countries continued to boom as more and more people left rural areas to live there. Eventually, larger cities such as London and New York developed a new urban/suburban pattern. Wealthier people have migrated to ever more distant suburbs, poorer workers have migrated to live in neighborhoods closer to the city center, and fewer and fewer people live in the city center itself. Many city centers have come to be used exclusively for industry and commerce—and eventually just for commerce, with industry clustered in zones along rivers or rail lines. This ever more expansive suburban sprawl has been made possible by automobiles, beginning in the United States as early as the 1920s and in Europe in the 1950s.

Population, energy use, and science and technology all boomed throughout the twentieth century, especially in the more-developed parts of the world. Combined, these factors enabled a great economic boom in the second half of the century. Much as the takeoff of industry in the 1800s was fueled by coal, so was this great economic expansion fueled by a tremendous increase in the use of petroleum. Oil was first pumped in Pennsylvania in the mid-1800s, but it wasn't much used until early in the twentieth century, and then it really took off after World War II, from 1950 to 1973. Then, the number of cars, trucks, and tractors fueled by petroleum exploded, even as new uses for petroleum (from airplanes to fertilizer to plastics) demanded more and more of it.

The rest of the world in many ways followed the European-American example of industrialization, urbanization, and population growth. But by the end of the twentieth century, it was clear that not all of those who lagged behind were catching up equally well. Latin America and East Asia, for example, have developed much more industry and trade with more-developed countries than most of Africa has managed. Furthermore, since about 1980, nearly everywhere, the richest one-tenth have become much richer while the poorest one-tenth have become poorer. With the end of the Age of Energy upon us, it's hard to imagine how those who are lagging behind will manage to catch up in the future.

And without a doubt, the Age of Energy–the era of cheap and plentiful fossil fuels–is coming to an end. We can argue about whether the world's production of petroleum has already peaked or will peak in a few years or a few decades, but sooner or later, that change will come. Like oil, other fossil fuels (coal, natural gas) and even the minerals we use for nuclear power are finite in supply. Long before we use them up completely, they'll become much more expensive and scarce, for we've already mined out their easiest and most profitable sources.

Making the inevitable transition beyond the Age of Energy is one of the greatest challenges humankind has ever faced. But it's not the only challenge we now face. In the next century, we'll see a change unheard of in human history since the adoption of agriculture set us on a course of ever growing population. That growth is now slowing. What happens when it stops?

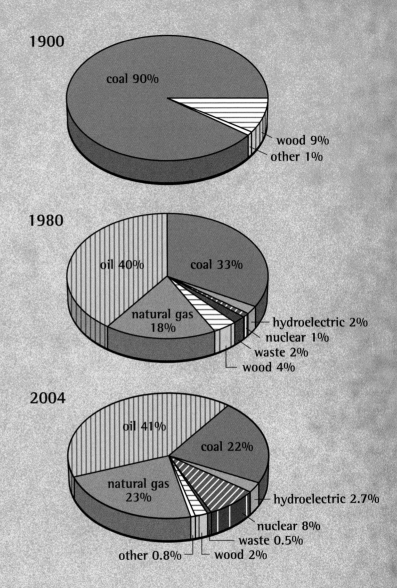

The world has seen a shift from almost total reliance on coal and wood at the beginning of the Energy Age to reliance on oil to fill nearly half of the world's energy needs. At the same time, the overall use of energy has greatly increased.

As Earth's population continues to grow and migrate toward dense population centers, solutions to the problem of overcrowding remain elusive. This image depicts one artist's vision of a city of the future.

chapter six

TWENTY-FIRST CENTURY

When social scientists want to look at how fast the population is growing, one number they look for is the total fertility rate, meaning the number of children each woman is expected to have during her lifetime. The "replacement" fertility rate (when population neither grows nor shrinks) is about 2.1 children per woman. Overall, the world's total fertility rate peaked about 1970. It is expected to drop to replacement level by or not long after 2050. After that, the world's population will continue to grow for some time, as the many, many children being born now grow up and have children of their own. Assuming, as looks likely, more and more women have children at or below the

WORLD POPULATION

TWENTY-FIRST CENTURY
2050 CE: 8.9 billion

AGE OF ENERGY
1850 CE: 1,260 million
1900 CE: 1,650 million
1950 CE: 2,520 million
2000 CE: 6 billion

AGE OF EMPIRES
1200–1400 CE: 400 million
1500 CE: 500 million
1750 CE: 790 million
1800 CE: 980 million

CRADLES OF CIVILIZATION
1000 BCE: 50 million
1–1000 CE: 300 million

AGRICULTURE 5,000 BCE
about 10 million

PREHISTORY 10,000 BCE
about 5 million

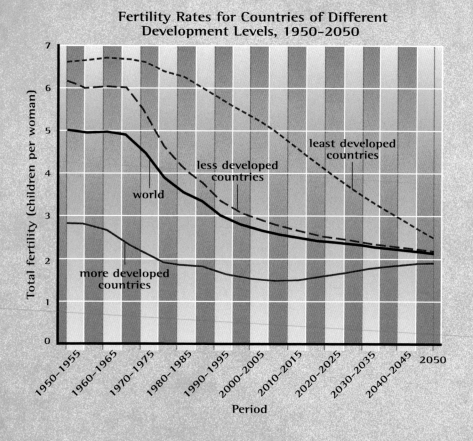

Fertility Rates for Countries of Different Development Levels, 1950–2050

Total fertility (children per woman)

least developed countries

less developed countries

world

more developed countries

Period

1950–1955 1960–1965 1970–1975 1980–1985 1990–1995 2000–2005 2010–2015 2020–2025 2030–2035 2040–2045 2050

replacement rate, the world's population will level off. Sometime in the next century, the growth in population that has been with us through all of human history will stop.

But while this is the overall pattern, the fertility rates and population totals for different parts of the world are and will continue to be quite different. This is because the reasons that lead to women having fewer children have reached the more-developed parts of the world before the less-developed regions. The first wave of those changes, related to industry and urbanization and improvements in health, reached more-developed countries early in the twentieth century, less-developed countries half a century or more later.

Similarly, a second wave of reasons why women are having fewer children (later marriages, more divorce, more use of birth control) reached more-developed countries by the 1970s and only thirty years later began to make a difference in less-developed regions. In addition, in dozens of the world's less- and least-developed countries, mostly in Africa, AIDS is expected to suppress population growth still further in the next half century.

The less-developed world's delay in trending toward a replacement fertility rate means that while more-developed parts of the world are already shrinking in population,

Source: United Nations Department of Economic and Social Affairs/Population Division, *World Population Prospects: The 2002 Revision* (New York: United Nations Publications, 2004), 3.

less-developed countries are still growing sharply. (Europe once again leads the trend. The United States continues to grow, chiefly because of immigration.) Over the next half century, nearly all of the world's projected population gain will be in urban areas of less-developed countries—with the sharpest growth in the world's least-developed countries. (These projections are based on best guesses about a lot of things, from access to birth control to the course of the AIDS epidemic. The overall number could be somewhat lower—or much higher.)

Less-developed countries with growing populations can expect worsening poverty and environmental

Baby Bonus Like most Western European nations, Italy's birthrate is so low that its population is shrinking and aging rapidly. The small town of Laviano decided to do something about it. In 2003 the town government began offering nearly $14,000 to the parents of every baby born there, paid out over the first five years of the child's life.

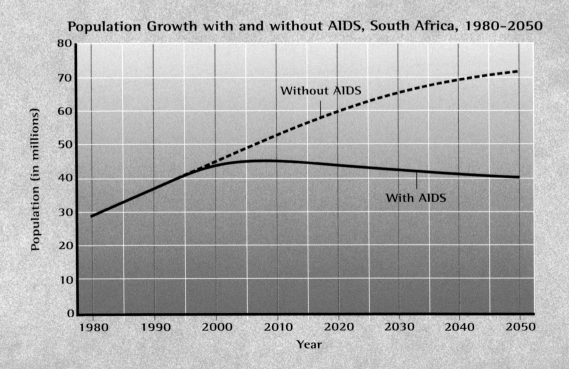

Population Growth with and without AIDS, South Africa, 1980–2050

To show how variables can affect population growth, the chart at left projects the population growth of South Africa as it would be if AIDS continues on its present course, and as it would be without the presence of the AIDS virus.

Source: United Nations Department of Economic and Social Affairs/Population Division, *World Population Prospects: The 2002 Revision* (New York: United Nations Publications, 2004), 14.

72 problems. Just feeding those growing numbers will be a great challenge. The vast increase in farmland since the 1980s is over. Because much of the land most recently turned to farming is in places not best suited for pasture or plow, and much more of all the world's farmland has been hard-used, the world is now seeing an overall loss of farmland (to desert, erosion, and other degradation) as well as a drop in the fertility of what remains.

The "constant" line projects population growth if the 2004 world fertility rate of 2.6 children per woman were to remain unchanged for the next 50 years. In the medium variant, fertility is projected to decline from 2.6 to slightly over 2 children per woman in 2050. The high variant indicates the world population reaching 10.6 billion by 2050, which is what would happen if the fertility rate were to reach half a child above the levels projected in the medium variant. The low variant tracks a fertility path half a child below the medium, which would lead to a population of 7.6 billion by 2050.

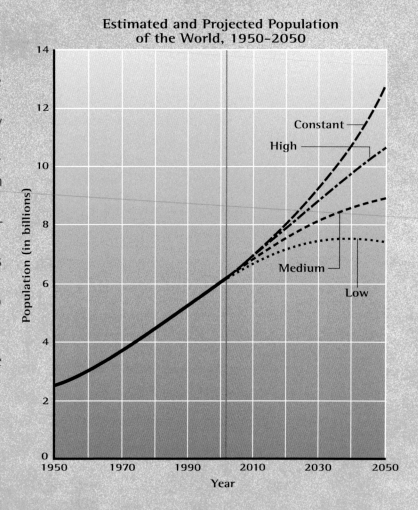

Estimated and Projected Population of the World, 1950–2050

Worse still, the great boom in the world's economy in the second half of the twentieth century was fueled by nonrenewable fossil fuels and driven by onetime events that can't be repeated: mass migration from farms to cities, the entry of women into the workforce, the spread of industry to the most populous of the world's less-developed countries (especially India, China and Japan), and economic gains from the "globalization" of trade. Even if all of these conditions persist, the great growth spurt of the past half century came from the change to the conditions– we've already made that

Source: United Nations Department of Economic and Social Affairs/Population Division, *World Population Prospects: The 2002 Revision* (New York: United Nations Publications, 2004), vii.

change now and can't repeat it. Nor are we likely to find other ways to keep economic growth going so fast, as population growth slows and supplies of fossil fuels and many other resources become scarcer and more expensive. For much of the twenty-first century, the less-developed world will almost certainly be pinched between a booming population and a slowing, or perhaps crashing world economy.

More-developed countries will have problems of their own. Dropping fertility rates (many more-developed countries are now well below replacement rate) combined with increases in how long people can expect to live mean more old people. The world's more-developed countries are aging fast, with fewer and fewer working-age people to support more and more elderly retirees. How will we support so many elders in a time of slow or no economic growth? No one knows what effects these differences between

MEDIAN AGE BY MAJOR AREA IN 1950, 2000, 2050 (ESTIMATED)			
	1950	2000	2050
World Total	23.6	26.4	36.8
More Developed Regions	28.6	37.8	45.2
Less Developed Regions	21.3	24.1	35.7
Least Developed Regions	19.5	18.1	27.1
Africa	19	18.3	27.5
Asia	22	26.1	38.7
Latin America and the Caribbean	20.1	24.2	39.8
Europe	29.2	37.7	47.7
North America	29.8	35.4	40.2
Oceania	27.8	30.7	39.9

Source: United Nations Department of Economic and Social Affairs/Population Division, *World Population Prospects: The 2002 Revision* (New York: United Nations Publications, 2004), 15.

Global Warming "The Earth's climate is nearing, but has not passed, a tipping point beyond which it will be impossible to avoid climate change with far-reaching and undesirable consequences. These include not only the loss of the Arctic as we know it, . . . but losses on a much vaster scale due to rising seas. Ocean levels will increase slowly at first. . . . But as Greenland and West Antarctic ice is softened and lubricated by meltwater, and as buttressing ice shelves disappear because of a warming ocean, the balance will tip toward the rapid disintegration of ice sheets. The Earth's history suggests that with warming of two to three degrees, the new sea level will . . . [be raised] by 25 meters, or 80 feet. Within a century, coastal dwellers will be faced with irregular flooding associated with storms. They will have to continually rebuild above a transient water level. This grim scenario can be halted if the growth of greenhouse gas emissions is slowed in the first quarter of this century."

—NASA scientist James Hansen, 2005

James Hansen, "The Tipping Point?" *New York Review of Books,* January 12, 2006, http://www.nybooks.com/articles/ 18618?email (June 14, 2006).

more- and less-developed regions will have on migration patterns in the twenty-first century. Already it's hotly debated what effects increased migration might have on the cultures of countries that either send or receive large numbers of migrants. From 1960 to 2000, between 2 and 3 percent of the world's population at any given time were international migrants, people living someplace other than the country they were born in. (Many more migrated within the same country.) But because the world's population increased so much during this time, the total number of international migrants increased from 75 million to 175 million. About three-quarters of these migrants made their way to the world's more-developed countries, with the United States accepting by far the largest number. Will the world's more-developed countries accept more migrants in the future, perhaps in part to add to the number of younger workers supporting older retirees? Which countries will decide not to do so, to avoid radically changing their culture by allowing so many foreigners to live among them? What will it mean in the future to be "French" or "German" or "American"?

In some ways, we're all migrants now. Modern communications and global media and pop culture now ensure that even people who stay in one place know much about the wider world that in the past only long-

distance migrants would have known. In the twenty-first century, will this knowledge 75
encourage more migration or less?

There's another way in which we're all migrants now: in our effects on nature. Humans and their creations and wastes now reach everywhere, all the time, with dire effects for many of the nonhuman creatures with whom we share our planet. Many scientists believe that Earth is on the brink of, or perhaps already well into, its sixth great mass extinction. In each of the first five extinction crises, more than two-thirds of the planet's species died out. (In the most recent, 65 million years ago, dinosaurs were among those that perished.) The current extinction crisis, if that's what it is, is the first to have been brought on or at least greatly influenced by human activities. Even if we're not (or not yet) witnessing the extinction of most species, there's no doubt that human activities from mining to farming to logging to industry have already extinguished countless forms of life and threaten many, many more. It's an open question whether the ultimate result of human migration and population growth, our expansion into every corner of our home planet, might not thus be the extinction of humankind as well.

However things turn out, the next century promises to be a time of dramatic transition for humankind.

SELECTED BIBLIOGRAPHY

The single most useful source for reliable, regularly updated information about human migration and population is the United Nations. Its various departments post a wealth of information online, at www.un.org. The UN publications most used in researching this book include: "2005 World Population Data Sheet," "World Fertility Report 2003," "World Urbanization Prospects: The 2003 Revision," and "World Population Prospects: The 2002 Revision."

Much of this book, especially the chapters on very early human history and on the twenty-first century, relied on newspaper and Internet accounts of very recent research. Both scholarship about the distant human past and projections about the future are changing rapidly; books dealing with these subjects can offer a good foundation but should be checked against more recent sources for updates. The following books are a good place to start for anyone who wants to look more deeply into human migration and population.

Cohen, Joel E. *How Many People Can the Earth Support?* New York: W. W. Norton, 1995.

Hollister, C. Warren, and Judith Bennett. *Medieval Europe: A Short History*. New York: McGraw-Hill, 2001.

McNeill, J. R., and William McNeill. *The Human Web: A Bird's-Eye View of World History*. New York: W. W. Norton, 2003.

Pagden, Anthony. *Peoples and Empires: A Short History of European Migration, Exploration, and Conquest, from Greece to the Present*. New York: Modern Library, 2003.

Ponting, Clive. *A Green History of the World: The Environment and the Collapse of Great Civilizations*. New York: Penguin Books, 1993.

Wells, Spencer. *The Journey of Man: A Genetic Odyssey*. Princeton, NJ: Princeton University Press, 2002.

Knapp, Brian J. *People of the World, Population and Migration.* Henleyon Thames, Oxon, UK: Atlantic Europe Publishing Co. Ltd., 1994.

Mason, Paul. *Population.* Chicago: Heinemann Library, 2006.

Spilsbury, Louise. *Moving People: Migration and Settlement.* Chicago: Raintree, 2006.

Woods, Michael, and Mary B. Woods. *Ancient Agriculture: From Foraging to Farming.* Minneapolis: Lerner Publications Company, 2000.

Zeaman, John, *Overpopulation.* Danbury, CT: Franklin Watts, 2002.

Websites

"Global Data Center," *Migration Information Source*
http://www.migrationinformation.org/GlobalData/
An interactive database that offers easy access to migration data and generates instant charts along the way.

"Human Population: Fundamentals of Growth; Effect of Migration on Population Growth," *Population Reference Bureau*
http://www.prb.org/Content/NavigationMenu/PRB/Educators/Human_Population/Migration2/Migration1.htm
A Population Reference Bureau site that explores the effect of immigration on population during the twentieth century.

"World Population Prospects: The 2004 Revision Population Database," *United Nations*
http://esa.un.org/unpp/
A United Nations-sponsored interactive database that will chart various population aspects of the world, as well as of many nations and regions.

INDEX

hunting, 12–13, 18–19, 21, 27–28

India, 34–35, 72
Industrial Revolution, 54, 56–57, 59–60
invaders, 35, 45
Islam, 46
Italy, 71

Jerusalem, 30

labor, specialization of, 31–32
language, 11–13, 14, 59
life expectancy, 65
London, England, 62, 66

Magellan, Ferdinand, 46
Manchester, England, 54
mastodons, 18
megafauna, 18–19
Mesa Verde (Colorado), 39
Mesopotamia, 22, 33–34
Middle East, 22, 24–25, 30
Minoan civilization, 35
Muslims, 46

national identity, 74
natural resources: conservation, 58; depleted, 38–39, 43; fossil fuels, 55, 56–57, 64, 66, 67; for industrialized nations, 62–63; trade in, 57–58

Neanderthals, 10
New Mexico, 19–21, 27–28, 36–39
New York, New York, 66
Nile River, 35

oil, 66, 67
Olmec civilization, 36
Oregon Trail, 53

Pakistan, 34–35
Paleo-Indians, 20
population: aging, 73–74; and agriculture, 27; and cities, 33; and climate change, 23; and disease, 44, 50, 51; in Dutch and British Empires, 48–49; in 1800, 50; and fertility rate, 65, 69–70, 73; and food supply, 13, 21; increased health of, 59, 65; and natural resources, 38, 43; projected areas of gain, 71–73; in Roman Empire, 43; slowing of growth, 65; in twentieth century, 63; in United States, 57, 58
Portuguese Empire, 46–47, 48
pottery, 28
public health measures, 65
Pueblo Bonito, 37
Pueblo peoples, 39

rainforests, 63
religion, 12, 32–33, 42, 45
Roman Empire, 35, 40, 42–45

savannas, 7, 8, 9
slavery, 50, 51
Spanish Empire, 47, 48
suburbs, 66
Sumer, 33–34, 35

Tehuacán Valley (Mexico), 29
tools, 6, 12–13
trade: early centers, 33–39; and exploration, 46–47, 48; in food, 31; in natural resources, 57–58; under Romans, 42; and slavery, 50, 51; and writing, 32;
transportation, 60, 63, 66

United States, 57–58, 74

wealth: and cities, 32–33; in Dutch and British Empires, 48–49; and industrial agriculture, 64; and Industrial Revolution, 58; and suburbs, 66
wood, 55, 56, 58
writing, 32

Zheng He, 50

80 ABOUT THE AUTHOR

Tricia Andryszewski has written twenty nonfiction books for children and young adults. She writes other work under the name Tricia Shapiro. A native of Pittsburgh and former resident of New York, New Jersey, Virginia, and Connecticut, she now lives in southern Appalachia.

PHOTO ACKNOWLEDGMENTS

Images in this book are used with the permission of: © Bettmann/CORBIS, p. 6; © Adam Jones/Photo Researchers, Inc., p. 8; © Mauricio Anton/Photo Researchers, Inc., p. 10; © Javier Trueba/MSF/Photo Researchers, Inc, p. 11; © HIP/Art Resource, NY, p. 18; © Warren Morgan/CORBIS, p. 20; © Ronald Sheridan/Ancient Art and Architecture Collection, Ltd., p. 22; © Vo Trung Dung/CORBIS SYGMA, p. 29; © The Art Archive/University of Coimbra/Dagli Orti, p. 30; © 2002 by the Regents of the University of Minnesota, Twin Cities. University Libraries, p. 32; © Dewitt Jones/CORBIS, p. 37; © MPI/Getty Images, pp. 39, 48; © North Wind Picture Archives, pp. 40, 53, 58; © Stock Montage/SuperStock, p. 42; © SuperStock, Inc./SuperStock, p. 47; © CORBIS, p. 51; © The Granger Collection, New York, p. 54; © Hulton Archive/Getty Images, p. 56; Library of Congress, p. 57 [LC-USZ62-93732]; © Stapleton Collection/CORBIS, p. 61; © Coneyl Jay/Photo Researchers Inc., p. 68. Maps, charts, and diagrams are by Laura Westlund/Independent Picture Service, pp. 12–13, 24–25, 34, 36, 43, 44, 45, 49, 52, 57, 60, 62, 65, 70, 71, 72, 73.

Cover illustration by Bill Hauser/Independent Picture Service.